DIALEC

BY

C000170665

BODY LANGUAGE 08

A MIDSUMMER NIGHT'S PRESS

New York

Main cover photo © Nir Arieli www.nirarieli.com

A Midsummer Night's Press
16 West 36th Street
2nd Floor
New York, NY 10018
amidsummernightspress@gmail.com
www.amidsummernightspress.com

Grateful acknowledgement is given to the editors of the
following publications in which some of these poems first appeared
(sometimes in a different form): *Gender Outlaws: The Next Generation*,
edited by Kate Bornstein and S. Bear Bergman: 'Shot, Stabbed,
Choked, Strangled, Broken'.

Designed by Aresográfico *www.diegoareso.com*

First edition, November 2012.

ISBN-13: 978-1-938334-00-9
ISBN-10: 1938334000

Printed in Spain.

CONTENTS

Resistance {5}

Wedding Poem {6}

Awkward {7}

Love Poem {8}

Annoyance {9}

Cunt {11}

Valediction {12}

For My Transdyke Sisters {13}

Tangle {14}

Crush {15}

Loving Despair {16}

Hatred {17}

23 {19}

Mirrors {29}

Calluses {30}

Transition {31}

Perspective {32}

Chair {33}

Privilege {34}

'My body is far older
than my skin' {35}

Chicago Legend 1978 {37}

Sonnet in Memory
of Steve Francis {38}

Shot, Stabbed, Choked,
Strangled, Broken {39}

Stonewall {43}

Pineapple {54}

Rubber {55}

Drag {56}

Dreamgirls {57}

Sore Throat {58}

L'Envoi {59}

Misrepresented {60}

RESISTANCE

You stroke my shoulder or my upper arm
in passing. Hardly pause as you walk by
but then look back and smile. Although I sigh,
shudder a moment, I remain quite calm,

you have not touched me deeper than my skin.
I tell myself breathe in and breathe again
after some small delay. I know the main
thing is to pass it off, and not give in.

You look so damned smug and I want to kiss
arrogance hard away from that soft mouth,
then kiss your neck and move my kisses south.
But I will not. And my best reason is

some lusts end up immortalised in song,
most start as muddle, then go badly wrong.

WEDDING POEM

These are all rituals – the catching sight
across a crowded room; the half-stroked wrist
during an introduction; not yet kissed,
the cheek inclined; the nervous overbite

and pout when nothing happens; the long talk
with friends about what may not have been meant
by words at parting; the lush flowers sent
to make things plain; and the extended walk

in seaside rain when something real is said
that can't be taken back. First kiss, first fuck,
first time you know that years of rotten luck
are over. These add up. Once you are wed,

they seem the tickings of a clockwork fate
that wound up from that first quite awkward date

AWKWARD

Love comes unasked for. Comes in the wrong year.
When you are busy, ill or slightly mad.
Reminds too much of bad affairs you've had
your lovers' similarities appear

at the worst moments. You look in the face
of some young thing and see behind her eyes
some ghost two decades dead. It's no surprise
this happens, for you always seem to chase

a certain turn of speech, angle of neck,
more than green eyes, firm breasts. They're not the same.
You must remember that. There is no shame
in having lists of things you have to check.

Yet sometimes, when love comes, you have to hurl
yourself into it, crazy for some girl.

LOVE POEM

You're out with someone else. They're smart and young;
they've ink on arms and lower back–a dove
drawn by Picasso. Later, they remove
the ribbons from their hair. And then their tongue

is on your shoulder blade; their fingers touch
the space between two ribs, and nestle there.
You wonder for a second if it's fair
and then you kiss them back. It is of such

moments that knowing you're in love is made,
because you break the kiss, and stroke their brow
like parents do. And then you wonder how
to do this kindly, then say 'I'm afraid

that this won't do.' They leave. You lie alone
and then call her you hope for on the phone.

ANNOYANCE

I really am too old for shit like this.
Strange bed, stale pillow, hair wrapped round my tongue.
Sore lips and yet no memory of a kiss.

They lie entwined. I need to take a piss,
I'll slip out from the sheets before too long.
I really am too old for shit like this.

My piss stinks and it makes a noisy hiss,
tried to be quiet but it came out wrong.
Sore lips and yet no memory of a kiss.

I woke from dreams of sex that seemed to miss
pleasure by miles. These girls are both too young,
I really am too old for shit like this.

Who dreams of bad sex? And my clitoris
stings like a bastard, echoes like a gong.
Sore lips and yet no memory of a kiss.

One of them fucked me in my sleep. That is
embarrassing and yet will make a song.

Sore lips and yet no memory of a kiss.
I really am too old for shit like this.

CUNT

The surgeons left me with a patchwork cunt,
stitch-marks and scars, and smooth skin flayed from thigh.
I bled. I oozed. With speculums, I'd try
to burn new keloids off. I'd grope and hunt

for small hard bits I'd missed. That now are smooth.
Things levelled out. You'd never know the sore
torn places that were there. For an old whore
it's sweet and neat and innocent as truth.

I paid in blood and pus. Here's what I got.
Not some mere hole, but tenderness. A maze
of flesh love's fingers have explored for days
and found its spring, gushing and furnace hot.

I dared not hope. Yet my reward was this—
to hang in ecstasy on sweet girl kiss.

VALEDICTION

I still have most of you. They changed your shape,
carved you and stitched you. Threw away my balls.
But when – as happens – someone hostile calls
what I chose mutilation, madness, rape,

I think unfondly of you. You'd go hard
when I was feeling tender, and would squirt
grey gunge like an eruption of wet dirt.
With you love, sex and gentleness were marred.

Yet now your strength gives tightness to each fuck.
Your thrilling nerves are rolled into a bud
that throbs. You still draw in a tide of blood,
I hear it roar and ebb and feel it suck,

gentle and overwhelming as the sea.
You're gone, but are still there, a part of me.

FOR MY TRANSDYKE SISTERS

Perhaps excessive neatness, or a scar
that spirals round the hood. You press your lips
against it, and she squirms up with her hips
and you lose track a moment. We all are

so prone to giggles of astonished joy
that what was hard won was a total gain.
Fingers force inner scars, a little pain
but worth it. She is wet. Let's not be coy.

Some of us love our sisters. On a date
saves time, we can avoid the big reveal.
They told us we were sick. Here's how we heal,
here's how those storms of self-contempt abate.

We bite and lick and groan in sweet surprise,
then check our lip gloss in each other's eyes.

TANGLE

The human heart is but a maze of meat
where muscle tangles in a gorgeous knot.
Red blood flows through it, lush and burning hot.
We wander through its paths on halting feet

whenever love begins. We feel its throb
quicken beneath us, troubling us again.
It is the one time that we welcome pain
we've felt before, we know that it will rob

our mind of dull staid, quicken each nerve,
quiver us into art. We feel the reins
that love pulls hard, our arteries and veins
harsh in our mouth. We're forced to make a swerve

where we would not have gone. Heart's such a bitch,
we know there's some new girl. We don't choose which.

CRUSH

Hold hands a moment, for a second touch
her cheek, picking a dead leaf from her hair.
Buy sweet red grapes for lunch, offer to share,
watch her mouth slowly crush them. It's too much

to hope for more and it is quite enough
to have these things, to have but not possess
her love, luxuriate in the distress
of stealing moments. Fragile and yet tough

wisps of desire. Accumulate your joy
fragment by fragment. Never say a word.
She's yours while she can say she never heard
a hint of what your actions speak. She'll toy

with you a month. Ten years from now she cries
awake from dreams of you, kissing her thighs.

LOVING DESPAIR

Despair, sweet mistress, could not be my muse
but kept me company until she came back;
whipped me with self-contempt–I heard ribs crack
as she trod down my breasts with iron shoes.

I could not sing of failure had I won
or know deep beauty without good looks' loss.
Threw dice–Despair had rigged my every toss.
Despair laughed at my empty purse, she thought it fun.

She promised much but proved to be a liar.
I bit my tongue in pain when my ribs broke.
I bled a while, tongue swollen. Then I spoke
new stronger verse. My muse and I conspire,

laugh last at my sad love, left bleeding where
I tore out verses when I screwed Despair.

HATRED

I feel them, looking daggers at my soul.
Women I'll never meet, have never seen,
who don't know all the places that I've been
that they've been too. And, really, on the whole,

perhaps it's best. I am a shabby rake,
no good example. Somewhere there must be
somebody who'd do better far than me,
convincing them their hate is a mistake,

somebody younger, smarter, lovelier far,
whose gorgeous dialectic of the skin
could both convince them and seduce them in
mere moments. But since such pure women are

above mere lust, she'd leave them to their hate,
come find me, maybe ask me on a date.

23

We all know how it works; we've read the books.
There are no whisperings across the years,
advising or consoling. Good job too.
Change one thing and the web of self is torn.
The world is sad enough without such tears.
You've read the books; we all know how it works.

You can't read this. It doesn't change a thing.
It's just a way of talking to oneself,
and not one's young self. There is no way back
but there's no real thing without pretence.
Pretence of which all memory is one.
It doesn't change the thing that you can't read.

You're twenty-three. There's books you haven't read,
not written yet, gadgets you've not switched on,
not yet invented. Not to patronize,
that is the hardest part. To keep in mind
the things you know, and didn't get from books.
The books you haven't read. You're twenty-three.

You're still a boy. You didn't mean to be
by now. You're scared of taking the wrong path,
of never moving, and of being poor,
of being killed. You need to take wrong paths.
You have to die to move. Right now although
you didn't mean to be, you're still a boy.

The plan was yours. You were the architect
who built a self that you could not yet see
from hope and fear. The stuff you didn't know
you made up; the things that you let go
built paths in time, lit bridges through the dark.
You were the architect; the plan was yours.

That year they put your friends behind the wire.
You spent your lunch-breaks leaning on a wall.
Your friends would cluster and you'd tell them tales
or sing or anything to keep them true.
The whole yard at their backs, that they'd ignore
to stay your friends, put there behind the wire.

The yard behind you, your side of the wall
echoed with fights and games, and no-one sang.
They'd pull you from the wire to stand in goal
or burn your wrist with gripping, twisting hands.
Your friends would wait and call and drift away,
leaving the wall, and you off in the yard.

Your father worried over how you walked
and would not let you act in the school play
for fear that they would cast you as a girl
and make him speak aloud the thought he feared
and start to lose the boy he'd dreamed you were.
And how you walked worried your father's dreams:

The Cubs, the Scouts, long walks and throwing balls.
He'd hoped that you could whistle, or see jays
that he'd point out. Still, you could manage knots,
tell tales of ghosts, cook pastry over fires,
or snare a rabbit. Not a waste of time,
long walks with him, thrown balls, the cubs, the scouts,..

Your father's scouting days were innocent.
He did not know what boys do in the woods
or how you built a dam and stood on it,
ten feet of water held back by your hand
to make the older boys leave you alone,
in innocence, like Father's Scouting days.

Helping to make bread god, in robes and lace,
passing the wine and oil, tinkling the bells,
knowing the words and sounding them so fast
the other servers wagered on your speed,
worries of flesh like cobweb torn aside,
spirit in robes and lace, to make bread God.

The scurf on old men's tongues, the reek of wine,
air stale with mothballs, caskets full of silks
and gold brocade that snagged a fingernail.
Driven away, the flesh will still return,
nagging till spirit blows away like foam.
The reek of wine, the scurf on old men's tongues.

Your virtue: irony in a friend's eye.
The more you knelt, walked Stations, told your beads,
Peter would snicker. He knew who you were.
The confidences of long walks to school,
the thoughts that hang where reticence betrays,
a friend's sarcastic eye watched you be good.

The name came first. You knew that it was yours.
You wrote that novel. (God, and it was bad!)
You let it go, and held the one true thing
the yellow notebook told. The girl was you.
The Rosalind you'd made up from yourself–
you knew that she was you. The name came first.

You read the books and they were full of fear.
Hugh Selby's Georgette had a rotten life.
John Rechy's Destiny was cute but strange.
'I want what I want' was not how you felt.
Anthony Storr said they and you were mad.
And you were full of fear from reading books.

The books taught many things apart from fear.
They taught you where to look. The bars. The street.
The street was kind to you. You were so young
and no-one hurt you. Ava, Sylvia—
both helped because you were their younger self,
afraid. Like books, they taught you many things.

Her house smelled of washed dogs and boiled cheap
                        meat.
Sylvia lived there and you went to stay.
She taught you makeup, how to be a whore,
but that you shouldn't have the life she had,
that you could have a different woman's life
that didn't smell. And where there were no dogs.

The bars were fun, though. Though you could not see.
Your glasses did not go with eyelashes.
Men said that you were pretty and you drank
the praise and drink they brought you, so you'd stroke
their cocks up backstreets, or in darkened cars
so they could not be seen. The bars were fun.

Those were weekends. You had to go to school,
a little stoned, with eyebrows that were plucked,
and no-one noticed, or perhaps they did.
The boys had pretty much all handled you.
They'd called it bullying, but it was sex.

You had to go to school. There were weekends...
You hope and pray. You never learn despair.
Your class mates dangled you above the street
and did not break or drop you. In the dark
you whispered prayers to silent apathy
all night, and still smiled in the morning light.
You never learned despair. You pray and hope.

You made those choices that you had to make—
The street, or Oxford. What you chose was hard,
The choice that gave more choice, the waiting choice,
To lie, and be, and not yet own the name,
And live in books and dreams and memories.
You had to make the choices that you made.

There is a lush life there behind your eyes,
a life you've stolen out of comic books,
from Chandler thrillers and from musicals
where you can twirl or pull a twenty-two
and kiss or blast those who are in your way.
Behind your eyes, the life you lead is lush.

Music has taught you how to live in times
where frenzy alternates with intellect.
Sweet flute is answered by dark trumpet call
and chaos turns to pattern. So you hope
for order out of tension and dismay—

to beat in time, the way that music taught.
Music and dreams. You sleep away the years
And hope to dream and not to choose.
Let friends harangue you, let them choose your name
until your sadness nearly broke your brain.
You weep, and choose. And wake out of the hurt
from years of sleep, and music, and of dream.

Nobody died yet. That changed everything.
Your heart's unbroken and you don't know loss.
You'll learn from time which rips and leaves a tear,
where there was love. Love is the only thing
that goes away and yet is always there.
Everything changes, though, when someone dies.

You find new bars, and streets that are less kind.
You can't pay back. Sylvia is not there.
You pay along, and help some younger friends.
Others you cannot help—drugs and despair,
police, rape, bad boys, and worse decisions, so
on streets even less kind, you find new bars.

The day you change, like any other day,
is sunny or is rainy. You get up
and put your new clothes on, and brush your hair
and put that on as well. Your breasts are sore—
they still have stitches. And you drink your tea

like any other day, the day you change.
The men you'll love are elegant and tall.
Arrogant, English. There'll be Alastair,
magic the only love he does not cheat,
that chokes him in the end. They are all bad
for you, and never going to be yours,
the elegant tall men whom you will love.

You nearly die. Parts of you rot away.
You burst an artery, and lie in bed
putting on weight from drugs that never work,
translating poetry to check your mind's
not turned to porridge. You learn to survive.
Parts of you rot away. You nearly die.

Men walk away. It's women who remain.
Women who fuck you near insanity,
women who bite and ask you for the whip
or flash their arse when you bring breakfast tea
or spoon against you in the dark of night.
Women remain. It's men who walk away.

You're on their list. There are so many lists.
You're stroppy, queer, demonically possessed,
a woman made not born, made by yourself,
born of yourself. You're not supposed to choose
and yet you chose, were born in blood and pain.

It's hard to list whose many lists you're on.
They don't kill you. And they don't kill your friends.
Shadows are dangerous for what they hide.
Hatred in boots, and knives that cut like words,
the words and knives that cut the years in half,
the time before, and time that had been cut.
Cuts that don't kill your friends, and don't kill you.

You have to trust life. When trust is betrayed,
build it again, look where you were the flaw
that broke the crystal. Look into the glass
and see your traitor face, your face betrayed
and know you are the crystal, and the flaw,
whose trust's betrayed. To live, you have to trust.

The woman you will be. She's quite the thing.
Not quite as pretty as you hoped to stay.
Much liked, a bit admired, and wrote some books.
Had heartbreak, broke some hearts, and stood up tall
for all that you believed in. You'd like her.
She's quite the thing, the woman you will be.

Horribly vain, as well, and greedy too.
Smug, slattern, feckless and a nasty tongue,
a gossip who plays games, but plays to lose
out of neurosis, never seeing through
the projects she begins. These are her faults,

she's greedy too, horribly vain as well.
Just to be fair, you have to see both sides.
You may think that the good outweighs the rest,
you might not. Of the faults, all I can say
is that you had to be there; of the rest,
that it was damned hard work to manage it.
You have to see both sides, just to be fair.

You're twenty-three. There's stuff you need to know.
Learning to let things go is one of them.
Let go to keep the moment fresh and fair.
Things are so fragile and so transient.
You hold them crystalled: let them fly away.
There's stuff you don't know yet. You're twenty-three.

MIRRORS

All mirrors lie. We look them in the eye
and they look back and say that we're no good.
Too old, too fat, too thin, too lame. We could
spend hours on self hate, but all mirrors lie.

The silver back to mirrors will betray
us if we let it. Every wise girl knows
the partial truth that any mirror shows.
We work around it and perhaps in play

we say oh well, perhaps my nose is big
but it has character. My waist is thick–
I'll stroke my warm curved flesh. I'm sick
of being told I'm bitch, or whore, or pig,

of feeling less than loved. I'll kiss the glass
and feel my own hands warm upon my arse.

CALLUSES

All bodies of my age are made of scar
and callus and the aching bit of bone
I broke at ten; my racing mind alone
is fresh, and yearning heart – such things as are

the vestiges of youth and can't sustain
youth's energy. Some say I pay the price
of holding on to youth. My heart breaks twice.
There are no calluses within my brain.

Just all the fresh and cutting wounds of lust.
My songs are made from pain and shame; I blush
at how I can still yearn, and can still rush
into Love's net of folly, can still trust

and stumble. Tripped. And manage to forget
pain past. I see Love's face, and still get wet.

TRANSITION

Boys eyes the glass where I could check my face
was on straight. And their pricks the long straight rule
to test my curves. I did not think to fool
and yet, finding myself in this new place,

I needed milestones. Found them in each bed
and then moved on. Then fate made me her bitch,
my tight dress tore with fat, stitch after stitch,
in months I counted by each turning head

that turned away from me. Now I am wise.
The love of women won by kindness, wit
and teasing's better than the useless shit
who fucks and leaves. Imagine my surprise

who learned from five short years, a surgeon's knife
lessons so cheap, they might have cost my life.

PERSPECTIVE

The past is mirrors, row on row at slants.
I walk upon the spot, hour after year,
and what will spark a smile, provoke a tear
is the half-sight, for seconds, in a glance

of my own younger face, and what I knew
or thought how much a mess my life would be.
And most of them are turned to misery
a few to crazy, can't believe it true

that I got through. Muddle, and drink, and pain
became the shining ink with which I write.
Wasted days moaning, lay awake at night.
Depression, wasted time, has turned to gain

I see those gloomy faces and I laugh
Life took so much, gave back all and a half.

CHAIR

I had a chair once. Cats had scratched its side.
I pushed the stuffing back and stitched it up
not all that neatly. Someone spilled a cup
of coffee down its back. The chair was wide

and comfortable, though I'd had to stack
cushions inside the seat where it had torn.
Lie back in it and you would start to yawn.
My body is that chair. Stuffed like a sack,

it sags in places, worn holes in its weave.
Its scars and stains the story of my days.
I'd never chose to cover or erase
those marks, but cannot let myself believe

that anyone would choose to snuggle here
or yawn or stretch or stay a week or year.

PRIVILEGE

My long thin skinny legs, arms without hair.
Nipples as large as eyes stared from my chest,
the faintest curve of what might be a breast.
One day my classmates tied me to a chair,

went to the blackboard, picked up coloured chalks,
rubbed blue above my eyes, red on my cheeks
and lips. The soreness stayed there for two weeks.
I'd often go for melancholy walks

out by the sewage farm and smell the shit
my life was then. Boys told me I was queer,
hang me from windows, stand around and jeer.
I was a freak, a girl, a thing, an it.

How can I trust women who say I'm hot?
Those sneering voices tell me that I'm not.

'MY BODY IS FAR OLDER THAN MY SKIN.'

My body is far older than my skin.
In lots of places, it's gone way past sag.
I wish I thought my beauty was within.

I know that vanity is called a sin.
I should be grateful that I'm not a hag.
My body is far older than my skin.

My hernia juts like a cooling fin,
I try to hide it with a shoulder bag
I wish I thought my beauty was within.

My creaking knee makes an appalling din
and if I dance or run it starts to nag.
My body is far older than my skin.

My hair's not silver – it is more like tin.
I wear a wig or wrap it in a rag.
I wish I thought my beauty was within

Some people would just soak themselves in gin

or drive around in an expensive Jag.
My body is far older than my skin.
I wish I thought my beauty was within.

CHICAGO LEGEND 1978

She was nineteen and pretty, wanted tits,
wanted them now and not to have to wait
for them to grow. Hormones take time and it's
so hard when you're with some guy on a date

and he finds padding. So she asked a friend
whose friend had talked to some guy that she knew
who'd shoot you up. She got someone to lend
most of his fee; when she got there, she blew

him for the rest. He stuck the needle in
and he screwed up. Some went into her heart,
some to her lungs. It really must have been
like drowning on dry land. You'd only start

to know you're dying when you fade to black.
He fed her to the dogs down at the track.

SONNET IN MEMORY
OF STEVE FRANCIS

Steve told me I would probably get fat;
'you'll hurt so much,' he said and worried that
I'd give up boys and turn into a dyke,
would stop being his friend, no longer like

the obscure broadway shows that he'd put on
when I went round. We'd have a marathon
of things that closed in days. 'And you won't fit
your Ossie Clark, the white one with the slit

that shows your legs.' He turned away and teased
his wig and fixed his lashes. I was pleased
he cared, and sad he didn't get it, so
I made excuses, really had to go.

Those were the last words either of us said
and I'm a fat old dyke and Steve is dead.

SHOT, STABBED, CHOKED, STRANGLED, BROKEN

a ritual for November 20th

1.

It could have been me,
I was young. I took risks.
True, I was white.
I hitched rides with guys.
One at least was a killer.
It could have been me.

It could have been me.
He came to my door.
He showed me a badge.
He pulled out a knife.
He raped me. I felt
the hilt of the knife.
I thought it the blade.
It could have been me.

It could have been me.
They beat me in the street.

They pummelled my breasts
and tugged at my wig
and said they would burn me.
It could have been me.

It could have been me.
He drew up alongside
and asked me to ride
and knew who I was.
He followed my cab
and drove his car at me.
It could have been me.

2.

They died
on the street corner with the streetlight that blinked,
with the rubbish bin dented by a passing car,
among bricks and bent girders,
on the waste ground behind the convenience store,
in the car park behind the bar where the toilets flooded
and the johns were bad men. Or in bed.
Their own bed where they thought they were safe.
They died where people who die by violence die.

They died because—
of course, there's no because. Just stupid whys.

They died for smiling the wrong way.
They died because god told someone gay things need to
               die.
They died because they answered back
or would not be called out of their names
or let his hand go there between their legs
or went on a hot date and told him and he didn't believe
               them until he did.
They died of other people's stupid violent hating ways.

The ones who died.
The ones we know about.
Thirty a year—that's more than two a month.
Handsome young transmen murdered in their pride:
Duanna, Angie, Kelly and the rest,
Iraqis with their long hair shaved away,
our sisters and brothers,
thirty of them,
dead

3.

When people die
their smiles are taken from us
who might have seen them
and smiled back.
Their songs are taken from us

who might have heard
and listened and been glad.
Their stories are remembered
by us, on this day
and always.

STONEWALL

1.

When there is a riot
is like
when there is a crisis
in a lot of lives.
It is when a hinge creaks,
when a hinge moves,
and things change.

The place
where there is a riot
where there is a crisis
That wasn't important
'til it was important.
Important for what happened there.

Stonewall
was just a bar
where gay men
and some dykes
went to drink

or to get laid.
It wasn't a bar
you went to
if you were
too poor, too queer, too young, too brown.
It was a bar
down the street.

One night
it was the place
where things changed.

2.

You have to remember,
you have to imagine,
you have to feel ,

how things were,
back in the day.

Some nights you went to a bar
and your life changed .
Not for the better.

The police would come in
because no one had paid them

or just cause they could.
And the police dragged you out.

You stood in night court
or lay in a cell
with drunks, hoods and thieves
who knew you were queer
and worse than they were
and no-one heard you scream.

The press took your name
and printed your name.
And that changed your life.

You lost:
your job,
your home,
the marriage where you hid,
your children and your future and your hope.

And people went to bars
for all the reasons people go to bars:
to drink, or to get laid.
And sometimes their lives changed.

That night
at the Stonewall bar

lives changed
and some for the better.

3.

We don't know all their names,
the people in the bar
when the police went in.
And then things changed.

So make them up.

Harold was there,
after the symphony
or after La Boheme—
he'd have to check...
He keeps his diaries still.
You don't call him Harry,
or Harriet,
he's Harold. Still.

He went there
because he wanted a drink
and wanted a fuck
and Judy had died
and he wanted a friend.

Arnie was there.
He worked construction,
he wasn't queer,
he told himself.
He wanted a blow job
and not to have to pay.

And Harold spoke to Arnie
and Arnie had a beer
and Harold had a white wine.
And then the police were there.

And Harold relaxed
and was sad about Judy
and dreaming of the man who got away
and Arnie thought well
I'm fucked
if this gets out.
On the construction site.

So Harold shouted: fuck off pigs!
and Arnie shoved a cop
and somebody hit Harold in the head
and Arnie said don't hit my friend.
And then it all kicked off.

Or, it wasn't quite like that.

It was Betty
who taught school
out in the suburbs
and was talking to Dean
who had an Elvis quiff
and could fix your bike better than any man.
And a cop told Betty he could fuck her better
and ran his fingers up and down her spine
and Dean said: fuck off pig!
And then it all kicked off.

Or it was Baby Val,
there for her birthday.
She was just eighteen.
The first time she'd been out
wholly in drag – and she just cried and cried.
The pigs had ruined her birthday.
So she cried.
And then it all kicked off.

4.

And so the police, they dragged
Harold and Dean
and Betty and Arnie and the rest
out of the bar and out into the street.
And then it all kicked off.

And they held Baby Val
inside for questioning.
And someone screamed
The pigs are beating Val in the back room!
And then it all kicked off.

The riot was the bar
and
the riot was the street.
The street where people lived.
The street where people walked,
too young, too queer, too poor, too brown.

Looking for handouts
or daddies for the night
or cheap street drugs,
in drag and out of it.

The people with nothing to lose.

I know their names
because they are my kind

Marsha P.Johnson–Present
Allyson Allante–Present
Tammy Novak–Present

Zazu Nova—Present
Birdy Riveira—Present
Storm Delaverie—Present
Miss Major—Present
Holly Woodlawn—Present
Sylvia Riveira—Present. Probably.
In spirit anyway.
So print the legend:
Sylvia was there
and maybe threw
the bottle-smash we hear around the world.

And all the rest:
Drag queens and street queens and hair fairies and gender
                    illusionists and Warhol superstars
Street Transvestite Action Radicals
(but that was later)
still they were all there.

In jeans that looked like you could peel them off
like fruit skin,
like peach skin,
like grape skin.
In eyeliner and eyelashes and paint
so thick it didn't crack,
so thick it didn't run,
tear gas made no impression on that slap.

And showgirl stockings
and their hair fluffed up.

Hurling dustbins
in high heels,
screaming screaming screaming queens.
We are the stonewall girls.
We wear our hair in curls.
We wear no underwear.
We braid our pubic hair.

And they were all so young:
Sylvia was seventeen,
sweet seventeen;
Allysson was fourteen,
parents threw trans kids away
so young back then;
Marsha was twenty five,
the oldest oldest lady on the street.

And it kicked off.
And Tammy ran away,
hid in Joe Tish's flat.
But she'd been there

And it kicked off.
And Holly got there late,

in time to throw a brick.
But she was there

They were the stonewall girls.
They wore their hair in curls.

They are my sisters, so I sing of them
like Homer did dead heroes.
And they're dead, the most of them.

Sylvia's liver went
when she was fifty.
Marsha, she was found
face down and floating.

Allyson's still here, married again,
and Holly, just about.
Sometimes trans folk make old bones.

The Stonewall girls,
their hair in curls.

Don't no-one ever say they were not there.

5.

This much we know:
That night everything changed
and they were there,
all of them, they were there.

The ones I know because they are my kind.
The ones I know because I made them up.

They changed their lives.
They changed all of our lives.

The hinge creaked
when the door opened.
The police came out of the bar
into the street.
And we came
out of the closet,
into the street.
Out of the closet,
into the street.
Out of the closet,
into the street.

PINEAPPLE

There is a ripeness on the brink of rot.
Beneath the rugged skin a hint of gray
softness that tells us in another day
flesh will be bitter. I would rather not

be ashes on a younger lover's tongue
and in her mouth decay to bitterness.
Some love affairs, so obviously a mess,
even to have that first screw would be wrong,

far better savour what will never be—
the scent, and elegant geometries
of skin—than see sharp anger in your eyes
that I've betrayed you, worse, that you've tricked me

and hate me because guilty. Rather flirt
and kiss, than fuck our friendship into dirt.

RUBBER

Her dress is red as blood pooled where the light
can make it glisten. Mischief in her eyes
more than allure, feigns innocent surprise
that we are looking at her. Latex tight

on skin. Her buttocks a pure aching curve
that eyes stroke, drawn there with a magnet's force.
We go on looking, even though remorse
is part of lust. Her naked arms deserve

a poem to themselves—they are that song,
extended line that covers yet implies
her breasts, just as the dress shows us her thighs
while hiding them. We know we do her wrong

in staring. She stares back. It's only just
that she should challenge our still-gazing lust.

DRAG

The most amazing drag queens haunt my sleep,
one in a black silk gown whose tight-cinched waist
implies that she's had several ribs replaced.
She's like two triangles. The two foot deep

white tangles of one's hair jut at the side,
flop at the front. It's like a Pekinese
were sitting there, and flopping at its ease
over her eyes. I really can't decide

what they are doing here. I think they're cool,
so stylish, so soigne and so bizarre.
There is a sort of beauty goes so far
(a geisha's eyebrows, dark lips of a ghoul)

it makes us think. Its glory is to dare
extremes, be great by simply being there.

DREAMGIRLS

I'd like to meet the girls I fuck in Dream.
The ones with leather dresses most of all,
who grope me in cafes and lick ice cream
between my breasts. I really wish they'd call.

I'd like to meet the older, wiser, cool
white trenchcoat-wearing gumshoe sipping gin
who sometimes shows. For her, I'd be a fool
for love, wild romance my besetting sin.

She could investigate me just as much
as she would like. But usually I wake
as lips stroke tongue. I'd like to stay in touch,
perhaps do brunch, if some of them could make

it to the daylight world where I forget
these evanescing cuties that I've met.

SORE THROAT

I love to hear you sing: rich, dark, and clear.
At best there's tattered velvet in my voice
that suits my verse. If I could have the choice,
I'd rather sing. Each has their own career;

we work with what we have. When I've a cold,
I work around it, slowly breathe, don't strain.
The catches in my throat are not a pain,
they are expressive. You, though, cannot hold

those perfect notes, if some quite minor bug
floods through your throat. And I will stay away
and save affection for another day.
Although I'm fond of you, we will not hug.

Or kiss. I'll walk away and not infect
the strong pure voice you've worked hard to perfect.

L'ENVOI

So, we are done. You hinted–I said no,
although my verses talk of might have been.
The things a cold observer would have seen
amount to little. You are free to go.

I wish you joy with him. I really do.
He's trim and buff and loves you. All I'll say
is, read my sonnets on some rainy day
years hence, and smile or weep. As to what's true

there's pose, pretense and sorrow, rhetoric,
rueful self-mockery. You're a coquette
whose lips and teeth and eyes I'll not forget
as they fixed on me. And I learned the trick

of verse that flirts straight back. Love him – be good.
You know I would have loved you if I could.

MISREPRESENTED

The woman that I love? She isn't you.
Although she has your dark curls in my head.
When people read the hurt words that I've said
and call you cruel, tell them it isn't true

that you said some harsh crass unfeeling thing.
It wasn't you, it was that bitch my muse.
I don't have to be sad, to sing the blues.
Nor be in love, exactly, when I sing.

Love unrequited, love on which I'll pass—
a useful fiction. It is poetry
that gets me wet. Be flattered when I lie,
imply it's you. Your cheekbones and firm arse

win rewards that last longer than a kiss:
Deathless with Laura, Lesbia, Beatrice.

ROZ KAVENEY is a middle-aged trans woman living and working in London as a writer, critic, and activist.

A regular contributor to *The Independent*, *The Guardian* and the *Times Literary Supplement*, she is the author of many books on popular culture, including *Reading the Vampire Slayer*, *Teen Dreams: Reading Teen Film and Television from 'Heathers' to 'Veronica Mars'*, *Superheroes! Capes and Crusaders in Comics and Films*, and *From Alien to the Matrix: Reading Science Fiction Film*, and a contributor to numerous reference works, including *The Cambridge Guide To Women Writing In English* and *The Encyclopedia Of Fantasy*.

She has recently published her first novel, *Rituals*, volume 1 of *Rhapsody of Blood*.

She was a co-founder of the Midnight Rose Collective, whose other members included Neil Gaiman, Alex Stewart, and Mary Gentle, which produced shared world anthologies including *Temps*, *Villains!*, and *The Weerde*.

She has also edited *Tales from the 'Forbidden Planet'* and *More Tales from the 'Forbidden Planet'*.

She helped found Feminists Against Censorship and is a past deputy Chair of Liberty (The National Council for Civil Liberties). She was also active in the Oxford Union debating society, the Gay Liberation Front, and Chain Reaction, a dyke SM disco she helped run in the 80s.

'I was reared Catholic but got over it, was born male but got over it, stopped sleeping with boys about the time I stopped being one and am much happier than I was when I was younger.'

Follow her blog at *rozk.livejournal.com* or her twitter @rozkaveney

A MIDSUMMER NIGHT'S PRESS was founded by Lawrence Schimel in New Haven, CT in 1991. Using a letterpress, it published broadsides of poems by Nancy Willard, Joe Haldeman, and Jane Yolen, among others, in signed, limited editions of 126 copies, numbered 1-100 and lettered A-Z. One of the broadsides—'Will' by Jane Yolen—won a Rhysling Award. In 1993, the publisher moved to New York and the press went on hiatus until 2007, when it began publishing perfect-bound, commercially-printed books, primarily under two imprints:

FABULA RASA: devoted to works inspired by mythology, folklore, and fairy tales. Titles from this imprint include *Fairy Tales for Writers* by Lawrence Schimel, *Fortune's Lover: A Book of Tarot Poems* by Rachel Pollack, *Fairy Tales in Electri-city* by Francesca Lia Block, *The Last Selchie Child* by Jane Yolen, and *What If What's Imagined Were All True* by Roz Kaveney.

BODY LANGUAGE: devoted to texts exploring questions of gender and sexual identity. Titles from this imprint include *This is What Happened in Our Other Life*, by Achy Obejas; *Banalities* by Brane Mozetic, translated from the Slovene by Elizabeta Zargi with Timothy Liu; *Handmade Love* by Julie R. Enszer; *Mute* by Raymond Luczak; *Milk and Honey: A Celebration of Jewish Lesbian Poetry*, edited by Julie R. Enszer; and *Dialectic of the Flesh* by Roz Kaveney.